Treasures of the
Series Three: Cultural Memory 4

Edited by Mary Boyle

Violent Victorian Medievalism

Text and translations: Mary Boyle.
Contributors: Emma Huber, Rachel
Delman, and Lucy H. Fleming. Poster
design: Katherine Beard.

Taylor Institution Library, Oxford, 2022

First published in 2022 by Taylor Institution Library

Copyright © Taylor Institution Library 2022

http://www.bodleian.ox.ac.uk/libraries/taylor

Exhibition funded by the Leverhulme Trust.

Images from Bodleian books produced by Bodleian Imaging Services and reproduced with permission.

Quotations from *Das Nibelungenlied*, ed. by Ursula Schulze (Stuttgart, 2020).

Cover image: 'The Slaughter in the Banquet Hall', Lydia Hands, *Golden Threads from an Ancient Loom. Das Nibelungenlied adapted to the use of young readers*, with fourteen wood engravings, by Julius Schnorr, of Carolsfeld (London, 1880), p. 61.

The online exhibition is available at https://violentmedievalism.web.ox.ac.uk.

Cover design: Emma Huber, Subject Consultant for German, Taylor Institution Library, based on the poster by Katherine Beard.

ISBN 978-1-8384641-0-3

Taylor Institution Library, St Giles, Oxford, OX1 3NA

Table of Contents

VIOLENT VICTORIAN MEDIEVALISM

Exhibition curated by Dr Mary Boyle | Leverhulme Early Career Fellow, Medieval & Modern Languages | Junior Research Fellow, Linacre College

Voltaire Room, Taylor Institution Library
7th & 8th Week, Michaelmas Term '22
Bodleian Library card required for entry

LEVERHULME
TRUST _____

Drinks reception & launch of the exhibition catalogue: December 2nd at 5 PM
REGISTER AT VIOLENTMEDIEVALISM.EVENTBRITE.CO.UK

POSTER DESIGN: KATHERINE BEARD

Poster designed by Katherine Beard, Linacre College, Oxford

Preface: Exhibitions at the Taylorian
Emma Huber

The Faculty of Modern Languages at Oxford University has an established tradition of using original library materials not only for research but also for teaching at all levels. The Taylor Institution Library works closely with academics and students, ensuring that acquisitions support their research interests and projects, and that our existing collections can be used to support outreach and engagement activities.

The Library supports scholars at all career stages to realise exhibition projects. The first booklet in this series was linked with an exhibition on the White Rose resistance group, curated by Early Career Researcher Alexandra Lloyd, which she has since developed into a research and engagement initiative: whiteroseproject.seh.ox.ac.uk/. Librarians provide guidance in the practicalities of preparing an exhibition, and help to promote it both online and within the library.

Exhibitions in the Taylor Institution Library are held in the Voltaire Room, a specialist reading room, and we are grateful for the patience of readers while exhibitions are set up, and while visitors look at the items on display. This exhibition on Violent Victorian Medievalism is the latest in a series of exhibitions curated by students and Early Career Researchers, and we look forward to many more.

Foreword: Medievalism in Oxford

Rachel Delman
Heritage Partnerships Coordinator, TORCH

Medievalism is ever-present in Oxford, a living heritage site. From the dreaming spires and the medieval traditions of the colleges to the rich archival and artistic holdings of the University's many libraries and archives, Oxford's visible medieval heritage continues to provide inspiration for academics, artists, creative writers and film makers to this day. Tourists flocking to the city are just as interested in medievalism as the medieval, as the existence of walking tours dedicated to C.S. Lewis, J. R. R. Tolkien and Harry Potter attest. The ways in which the Middle Ages are continually remade and unmade tell us as much about our present as our past. Collaborative initiatives exploring medievalism in the form of exhibitions and heritage interpretation are therefore key to understanding what we choose to remember (and, just as importantly, forget), and why, as well as how, we situate ourselves in the city, and the world, around us.

Contributors

<u>Mary Boyle</u> is the curator of the exhibition and the catalogue editor. She is a Leverhulme Early Career Fellow in the Faculty of Medieval and Modern Languages, and a Junior Research Fellow at Linacre College. Mary's current research project looks at cross-cultural medievalism in the long nineteenth century (1789-1914), focusing on the ways in which anglophone writers translated and adapted medieval German literature, and German-speaking writers translated and adapted medieval English literature. Mary's recent publications include *Writing the Jerusalem Pilgrimage in the Late Middle Ages* (D.S. Brewer, 2021) and *International Medievalisms* (D.S. Brewer, 2023).

<u>Katherine Beard</u> designed the exhibition poster. She is currently working on a DPhil combining the study of the Old Norse mythological literary corpus with the analysis of Viking Age artifacts. Upon completing her MA in Old Nordic Religion from the University of Iceland, she published the accompanying Eitri database (eitridb.com), a novel digital-humanities platform that houses several hundred individual Þórr's hammer amulet finds. Her DPhil research expands this database to include other Viking Age objects of power like the sword, spear, cup, and chairs, and puts them in context with their medieval literary counterparts to tease out new conclusions.

Rachel Delman has written the catalogue foreword. She is the Heritage Partnerships Coordinator in the University of Oxford's Humanities Division, and has recently returned to Oxford after research fellowships in Edinburgh and York. Rachel's recent publications include 'The Queen's House before Queen's House: Margaret of Anjou and Greenwich Palace, 1447-1453' in the *Royal Studies Journal*, 8/2 (2021), for which she won the Royal Studies Journal Article Prize (2021) and the Richard III Society research prize (2022). Her monograph on elite women's residences in late medieval and early Tudor England is forthcoming with Oxford University Press.

Lucy H. Fleming contributed the essay 'Safe and Unsafe Violence in Victorian and Edwardian Children's Chaucers'. She is a doctoral candidate at New College, Oxford. Her dissertation explores the poetics of adaptation in children's prose retellings of Chaucer and Shakespeare, with a focus on sexuality, obscenity, and temporality.

Emma Huber has written the catalogue preface, designed the cover, and provided invaluable support for the exhibition's development, curation, and logistics. She is the Subject Librarian for German at the Taylor Institution.

Violent Medievalism, Violent Victorians

Mary Boyle

medievalism, *n.*

'the reception, interpretation or recreation of the European Middle Ages in post-medieval cultures'

Louise D'Arcens, 2016[1]

A portcullis creaks. Dismembered corpses litter the snow. An unwashed man dismounts and looks on in terror. Just minutes into the first episode of *Game of Thrones* (HBO, 2011–19), the scene is set. This world, visually coded as medieval, is brutal. Such a trope crops up again and again in contemporary popular culture, often clearly taking a lead from HBO's era-defining series. Even puppets were beheaded in the teaser for *The Green Knight* (A24, 2021), while trailers for other medievalist films and television programmes over the past decade repeatedly emphasise barbarity and bloodshed: *Vikings* (History, 2013–), *The Last Kingdom* (BBC, Netflix, 2015–), *Outlaw King* (Netflix, 2018). One of the latest iterations is called, simply, *Medieval* (WOG FILM s.r.o., 2022). But despite defending the violence in *A Song of Ice and Fire/Game of Thrones* by saying, 'It's not the Disneyland Middle Ages', George R.R. Martin did not rip the Band-Aid off a shared vision of a utopian Middle Ages to reveal historically accurate and hitherto unexplored gore. In truth, the idea that 'medieval' is a synonym for violent, even when not explicitly articulated, runs through later responses to the period, from the cerebral to the popular.

Enter the Victorians. A fascination with the Middle Ages shaped public life in the nineteenth century—and in exchange, it reshaped the Middle Ages into a form still dominant today. Englishness became inextricably connected with a reimagined medieval past expressed through art, architecture, and literature. English traits and values were traced to a Golden Age of chivalry, and a national character was anchored in a heroic so-called Germanic past (also described as Anglo-Saxon, Northern, or Teutonic). The longevity of this tradition is evident in the 2021 St George's Day Google Doodle.[2] But chivalry and heroism necessarily exist within a martial context, and violence already permeated the geopolitics, literature, and culture of Britain's 'imperial century'. Abroad, Britain added 400 million people and 10 million square miles to its Empire, at the cost of countless lives.[3] At home, cheap and garishly illustrated penny dreadfuls sold in huge numbers thanks to rising literacy rates and an increased appetite for entertainment.[4] This taste for melodrama gave rise to the sensation novel which—supposedly—had a more respectable audience. It catered, though, to an equivalent taste for bloodshed.[5] Medieval or medieval-adjacent literature offered another respectable vehicle for violence. In the 1830s, Thomas Carlyle published an essay drawing the nation's attention to a medieval epic, 'belong[ing] especially to us English *Teutones*'.[6] This was the *Nibelungenlied*, a story of love, betrayal, vengeance, and hopeless heroism. It had already been decreed a potential 'German *Iliad*'—and, like the *Iliad*, its body count was vast.[7] With its frequent scenes of graphic violence and potential for ethnonationalist identity construction, the narrative incorporated various national pursuits for the Victorians. They revelled in it, as did the Edwardians—right up to the First World War.

'The hostel in flames' (detail) Lydia Hands, *Golden Threads from an Ancient Loom. Das Nibelunglied, adapted to the use of young readers*, with fourteen wood engravings by Julius Schnorr, of Carolsfeld, London, 1880, p. 66.
Private loan.

***

The *Nibelungenlied*

Uns ist in alten mæren wunders vil geseit
von helden lobebæren, von grôzer arebeit,
von fröuden, hôchgeziten, von weinen und von klagen,
von küener recken strîten muget ir nu wunder hœren sagen
The Nibelungenlied, stanza 1

In ancient tales, we are told much of wonder: of praiseworthy
heroes, of great toil, of joys, festivals, of tears and laments, and of
brave warriors battling, now you may hear wonders told.

The *Nibelungenlied* is the most famous German version of a collection of heroic legends known also in various Scandinavian incarnations. It tells of the dragon-slaying hero Siegfried and his arrival in Burgundy, where he hopes to woo the famously beautiful Princess Kriemhild. Various obstacles—or opportunities to prove himself—present themselves. He fights off invading Danes and Saxons and, through dishonest means, helps Kriemhild's brother Gunther win the hand of the warrior queen, Brünhild, after which Siegfried and Kriemhild are also married. Years later, while Siegfried and Kriemhild are visiting Burgundy, tensions erupt, and Gunther conspires with his vassal, Hagen, to have Siegfried murdered. Hagen stabs him in the back while they are hunting in the forest, and leaves his body outside Kriemhild's door. Hagen then steals her treasure hoard, a gift from Siegfried, and sinks it in the Rhine, ostensibly to prevent her from using it to gain allies in pursuit of revenge.

Years pass, and Kriemhild accepts a marriage proposal from Etzel, King of the Huns, hoping to find an opportunity to avenge Siegfried. She invites the Burgundians to visit her and engineers an outbreak of violence. Ultimately, almost nobody is left alive, and Gunther and Hagen, the last surviving Burgundians, are brought before her. She orders her brother to be killed and brings his head to Hagen, before decapitating Hagen with Siegfried's sword. A bystander, outraged that this fearsome warrior has been killed by a woman, strikes Kriemhild down himself, and the poet concludes:

> Ine kan iu niht bescheiden, waz sider dâ geschach,
> wan ritter und vrouwen weinen man dá sach,
> dar zuo die edeln knehte, ir lieben friunde tôt.
> dâ hât daz mære ein ende. diz ist der Nibelunge nôt.
>
> *The Nibelungenlied*, stanza 2376

> *I cannot tell you what happened there later, only that knights and*
> *ladies were seen weeping, noble squires too, their dear friends dead.*
> *Here the story has an end: this is the Nibelungs' distress.*

***

After Carlyle's essay, anglophone adaptations began to appear, initially as a trickle and then, following the first performances of Richard Wagner's *Ring des Nibelungen*, as a flood. Writers often adapted not only the *Nibelungenlied* itself, but combined it with the other Scandinavian and German narratives associated with its characters, and introduced elements from their own imaginations—

just as Wagner had done. The resulting adaptations were aimed at all age groups and educational levels, and many were eye-catchingly illustrated. While the slightest allusion to sex was usually avoided in Victorian and Edwardian adaptations (as opposed to translations) of this material, gruesome violence tended to make it through, including in those versions aimed at children. Indeed, it often appeared in picture form: a woman brandishes the decapitated head of her brother; a man is stabbed in the back while drinking from a spring; a knight faces up to a fearsome dragon. Some illustrators stopped short of depicting the violence itself, but were happy to depict the moments immediately before or after: the spear poised to leave a hand and enter a back; piles of corpses. This predilection for carnage has echoes of modern children's educational entertainment like *Horrible Histories* (CBBC, 2009–2020, based on Terry Deary's book series, 1993-2013), which was marketed as 'history with the nasty bits left in', but it was also par for the course in the long nineteenth century (1789–1914), and was certainly not limited to the items on display in this exhibition. Lucy H. Fleming's contribution to the catalogue on children's adaptations of Chaucer, for example, casts light on another tradition of medievalist violence in the nineteenth century.

The *Nibelungenlied*, along with its associated material, however, was so widely reinterpreted in the long nineteenth century, and so emblematic for notions of a so-called Germanic identity, that it provides a useful prism through which to demonstrate the wider implications of violent Victorian (and Edwardian) medievalism.[8] Children's literature of this period routinely matched a reticence about sex with scenes of extreme violence, often while simultaneously smuggling in an educational message. In adaptations of the *Nibelungenlied* and other related legends, that message was unequivocal, both for children and for adults: this narrative is your cultural inheritance. We can thus see the connection forged between (ethno-)nationalist nostalgia and a violence that can often be parsed as heroic or fantastical, thus neutering potential charges of sensationalism. It is a clear forerunner of twentieth- and twenty-first-century children's medievalism, as well as mapping on to more recent trends in violent medievalism and popular culture.

The Taylorian exhibition is accompanied by an online exhibition, which can be accessed at https://violentmedievalism.web.ox.ac.uk.

Notes

[1] Louise D'Arcens, 'Introduction: Medievalism: scope and complexity', in *The Cambridge Companion to Medievalism*, ed. by Louise D'Arcens (Cambridge, 2016), pp. 1–13.

[2] '23 April 2021: St. George's Day 2021', *Google*, 2021 <https://www.google.com/doodles/st-georges-day-2021> [accessed 29 September 2022].

[3] Timothy Parsons, *The British Imperial Century, 1815-1914: A World History Perspective* (Lanham, Boulder, New York, Toronto, and Oxford, 1999), p. 3.

[4] For more information on the penny dreadful, see Judith Flanders, 'Penny

Dreadfuls', *British Library*, 2014 <https://www.bl.uk/romantics-and-victorians/articles/penny-dreadfuls> [accessed 29 September 2022].

[5] For more information on sensation novels, see Matthew Sweet, 'Sensation Novels', *British Library*, 2014 <https://www.bl.uk/romantics-and-victorians/articles/sensation-novels> [accessed 29 September 2022].

[6] Thomas Carlyle, 'Das Nibelungen Lied, übersetzt von Karl Simrock (The "Nibelungen Lied", translated by Karl Simrock.) 2 Vols. 12mo. Berlin. 1827.', *Westminster Review*, 15/29 (1831), p. 4.

[7] Johannes von Müller, *Der Geschichten schweizerischer Eidgenossenschaft. Anderes Buch. Von dem Aufblühen der ewigen Bünde* (Leipzig, 1786), II, p. 121.

[8] Because such tendencies continue beyond the strict boundaries of the Victorian era, as far as the outbreak of the First World War, the exhibition includes items published up to twelve years after Victoria's death.

Translating Violence: the *Nibelungenlied* for Children

Mary Boyle

The original version of this piece was originally published on the Queen's Translation Exchange blog (www.queens.ox.ac.uk/translationexch-blog) in 2021 as 'Translating Medieval Violence: What's Acceptable for Children?'.

Knights and dragons are such a fixture of children's literature that they seem to find their way into the least medieval settings imaginable. Not only is there even a *Postman Pat* episode on the topic but, since I started writing this, I've discovered that there are two ('Postman Pat and the Greendale Knights' (2007) and 'Postman Pat and the King's Armour' (2017)). But have you ever stopped to think about how strange this is? Dragons are bloodthirsty monsters, while the business of knights is, well, violence. It might be characterised as violence in the service of their country, or to protect damsels in distress, but it's violence nonetheless. The purpose of those swords isn't simply to shine, but to kill—or at the very least to threaten to kill. And yet we think of these characters as not just child-friendly, but obvious material for children's stories. Why?

Fitting knights and their world into children's literature isn't a new idea, but goes back well over a hundred years, to Victorian and Edwardian children's authors who made use of medieval texts in their search for new material for young audiences. Drawing on the past is never politically neutral, and it certainly wasn't for these writers, who were getting involved in a contemporary passion for the Middle Ages which was so influential that many of the things we think of today as medieval are actually products of the nineteenth century.[1] So why wasn't this politically neutral? Countless words have been written about this, but to cut a long story short and then simplify it, there was a desire to identify the beginnings of English culture and democracy in a pre-Norman-Conquest past which was shared with other supposedly 'Germanic' (itself a complicated and loaded term) regions like Germany and Scandinavia. Given this background, maybe it's not surprising that writers at the time decided that the *Nibelungenlied* would make a perfect children's book. After all, it featured not only those knights and dragons, but also other fairy-tale staples like kings, queens, princes, princesses, treasure, prophecies, and battles.

Unfortunately, the *Nibelungenlied* also has pretty non-child-friendly features: sex and sexual violence; betrayal and (mass) murder; the decapitation of a child; burning people alive; drinking blood from corpses; the parading of the decapitated head of one prisoner in front of another; the beheading of an unarmed man; and—to close proceedings—the brutal killing of a woman. Basically, the knights behave like the warriors they are—but it's worth pointing out that, generally speaking, the violence itself wasn't exactly a problem for our writers. The real issue was that much of the violence is directed (and partly carried out) by a woman, our main character, Kriemhild.

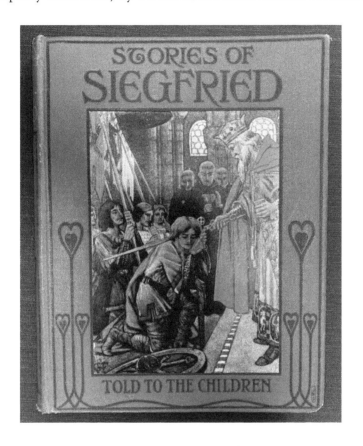

The cover of a later children's adaptation of the *Nibelungenlied*
Mary MacGregor, *Stories of Siegfried, told to the children*, with pictures by Granville Fell, London, c. 1908.
Private loan.

Turning the *Nibelungenlied* into a children's story obviously wasn't going to be just a matter of translating it from Middle High German into English and putting it in the hands of young Victorians. The mostly fairy-tale-like first half of the narrative was quite easily adapted for children, but the second part presented many more problems because the plot basically follows Kriemhild's violent quest for revenge. Now admittedly, it could have been worse—the Scandinavian material features the female protagonist killing her children, baking them into pies, and serving them to their father. At least Kriemhild's limit was putting her son in a situation which she knew would lead to his death in order to further her revenge plot. One common solution was to adapt only the first part, perhaps summarising the revenge plot in a few sentences. These adaptations would usually bring in some Scandinavian material, which had the advantage over the German version that the fight with the dragon didn't take place 'offscreen'. This particular violence only involves a man and a monster, so it could appear in its full gory detail, including Siegfried's post-fight bath in the dragon's blood. But there were some writers who decided that they were just going to go for it and adapt the whole thing. Let's take a look at two of them.

First up, Lydia Hands, author of *Golden Threads from an Ancient Loom*, subtitled *Das Nibelungenlied, adapted to the use of young readers*. She was ahead of the curve by publishing in 1880—most English-language children's adaptations of the *Nibelungenlied* came along after the English premiere of Wagner's *Ring* cycle in 1882 drew attention to the material. Hands deals with the difficulty of translating Kriemhild's violence by finding an explanation which would make (legal) sense to her audience: Kriemhild was mad with grief at the death of her child. You're probably thinking that this is a bit rich of Kriemhild, since this is entirely her own fault. So Hands simply neglects to translate that part of the text. In her version, the boy's death comes as a terrible shock, causing Kriemhild to faint in horror. When she wakes up, 'a frenzy, as of madness, possessed Criemhild; her enemy should not escape, even though her own life should be the penalty'. Then she orders the hall to be burned down with hundreds of men inside. It's the death of her son that triggers Kriemhild's madness, and her madness which triggers her indiscriminate violence. Insanity was a routine defence in nineteenth-century law courts, and it means that Hands can keep all the violence—and she *really* does—without undermining contemporary expectations of women. It doesn't excuse Kriemhild, and she doesn't get a happy ending, just a marginally less violent death, but it relieves her of her moral responsibility and any knock-on consequences for society.

This wasn't enough for Gertrude Schottenfels in *Stories of the Nibelungen for Young People* in 1905. There's no violent death for Kriemhild's son, and Kriemhild herself is kept at some distance from the violence. Eventually, Hagen and Gunther are brought to her by a knight, who makes her give 'her word of honor that he, and he alone, should be permitted to put them to death'. So really, when Kriemhild orders them to be beheaded 'according to the custom of these olden times', she's just following a knight's suggestion. This Kriemhild is allowed to live, and the closest we get to a condemnation is being told that she was 'once gentle and beautiful', implying that she no longer is. But she's neither dead nor disgraced, and the spectacular body count isn't attributed to her.

Maybe this is as close as we get to an answer to my starting question. Compared to the other violence in the *Nibelungenlied*, knights' (and dragons') violence isn't considered a big deal. As long as you can translate away the unacceptable violence, you can keep the rest—no matter how extreme.

Images from Lydia Hands' *Golden Threads from an Ancient Loom* are on display in this exhibition.

---

[1] For more on this, see my blogpost 'The Medievalism Onion: Layers of Interpretation', *TORCH*, 2020 <https://www.torch.ox.ac.uk/article/the-medievalism-onion-layers-of-interpretation> [accessed 14 October 2022].

Safe and Unsafe Violence in Victorian and Edwardian Children's Chaucers

Lucy H. Fleming

Those who decry any form of violence in children's literature and media would no doubt disapprove of swathes of Victorian children's fiction, especially the notoriously violent stories targeted at boys. Buoyed in part by Christian reformist movements, the later Victorian period saw a somewhat unexpected alternative to these 'penny dreadfuls': retellings of classic English texts, including Geoffrey Chaucer's *Canterbury Tales*. Like the children's Shakespeares that predated and partly inspired them, children's Chaucers appealed to educators as well as to parents, offering a carefully curated introduction to the 'Father of English Poetry' that promised to help child readers 'become wise and good, by example of the kind creatures' in the stories.[1] But to children's adapters, the *Tales* posed a hefty challenge, not least because a staggeringly low proportion of Chaucer's characters are demonstrably 'wise', 'good', or 'kind', as claimed. The fourteenth-century *Tales* are rife with incidents of mutilation, murder, and physical abuse, not to mention sex, flatulence, adultery, and child marriage. As such, their afterlife in children's adaptation is a rich case study for thinking about how medievalist Victorian children's literature balances its competing agendas: presenting a compelling, 'authentic' version of the medieval while simultaneously rendering it 'safe' enough for the genre's 'delicate' readership. Given the content of the source material, children's Chaucer might be as paradoxical as the idea of 'safe violence', but Victorian and Edwardian children's adapters tackled Chaucerian violence in both predictable and unexpected ways as they crafted their 'impossible story-book[s]'.[2]

Children's adapters were certainly aware of the 'coarseness' of some of Chaucer's tales, and their first and bluntest adaptational tool was that of omission. Twenty-two children's Chaucers were published between 1837 and 1914, and none adapt the *Tales* in their entirety. While bawdiness immediately disqualifies several tales, violence also plays a role; specifically, violence against or perpetrated by women makes a tale far less likely to be adapted. By contrast, violence between men appears 'safe' enough to feature in both of the most popular tales of the period: the Nun's Priest's Tale, which stages an attempted murder made comical by the cast of barnyard animals, and the Knight's Tale, with its chivalric pageantry.

The Knight's Tale in particular is worth a closer look if we want to understand how violence 'safely' makes its way to the page. The Tale contains some of the most graphic descriptions of physical violence in Chaucer's corpus, as in this moment when the characters Palamon and Arcite duel:

> As wilde bores gonne they to smyte,
> That frothen whit as foom for ire wood.
> Up to the ancle foghte they in hir blood.
> > *The Canterbury Tales* (*CT*), lines 1658–1660 [3]

> *They began to smite as would wild boars*
> *That froth white as foam with anger.*
> *They fought up to the ankle in their blood.*

Appearing more than twenty times, *blood* dominates the Knight's Tale: found 'with many a grevous blody wounde' *CT*, 1010), it is Palamon and Arcite's 'blood roial' (*CT*, 1546) that saves their lives, and their intimacy and blood relation that makes more tragic their fatal competition for the same woman's hand in marriage. But in children's adaptation, blood is almost nowhere to be found. Consider R. Brimley Johnson's 1909 version of the above lines:

> They smote each other like wild boars in their mad anger.
> And so I leave them while I tell you of Theseus…[4]

Johnson closely paraphrases Chaucer's chivalric animal imagery, but omits the sudden reminder of the fight's ugliness and gore. Notably, those that *do* include the blood in this moment are writing for an audience of boys, for example, 'Long they fought, until at each step they sunk ankle deep in blood'.[5] Like Johnson, other children's adapters typically hew closely to Chaucer's narrative when it comes to violent acts between men—for instance, the killings in the ever-popular Pardoner's Tale—but render them safe by omitting the grisliness of open wounds and bodily fluids.

'Fighting furiously as two wild boars.'

Note the lack of contact and lack of blood in Palamon and Arcite's duel, even as they are 'fighting furiously as two wild boars': F.J. Harvey Darton, *Tales of the Canterbury Pilgrims: Retold from Chaucer & Others*. Illustrated by Hugh Thomson. London, 1904, repr. 1906, p. 35. Courtesy of Toronto Public Library.

The absence of blood in children's adaptation also bears on the issue of gender within the text, as when Chaucer's Emelye, having prayed to the goddess Diana to grant her wish to stay a virgin and never to marry, witnesses a burning branch throw sparks '[a]s it were blody dropes' (*CT*, 2340) — a portent, possibly, of Arcite's impending death. Predictably, Victorian children's adapters omit this blood as well, but they also omit the specifics of Emelye's prayer—or the entire prayer itself. And nowhere is the contrast between handling of sex and violence more stark than in the descriptions of the three temples in the Knight's Tale—for Venus, Mars, and Diana, respectively. Chaucer's loquacious Knight relishes his descriptions of these ornate buildings, giving detailed descriptions of their furnishings and décor. Children's adaptations cut short much of the lengthy description, but do so disproportionately. Mary Seymour, for instance, reduces the temple of Venus, with its Chaucerian nude statue and frescoes of consensual and non-consensual 'lustynesse' (*CT*, 1939) to 'paintings of feastings and dancing', but retains the violent imagery of Mars' temple.[6] Of the three temples, Diana's typically receives the least fanfare. In children's adaptation she is merely the goddess of hunting, and the violence of her temple—which in Chaucer includes her effective murder of Actaeon and a brutal depiction of childbirth—is completely erased. Again, adaptations sanction the male-dominated violence of formal war and physical altercation but deem violence perpetrated by or suffered by women 'unsafe' for their readership. In so doing they reinforce, like many other children's adaptations, a conservative approach to gender roles even as they might claim to protect their vulnerable female readership.

The gendered 'safety' of violence manifests most strikingly in adaptations' handling of what appears to be the ultimate taboo in children's adaptation: rape. As mentioned, tales involving explicit violence against women are usually omitted. The major exception is the Wife of Bath's Tale, which opens with a scene of unmistakeable rape but which proved remarkably popular during the Victorian and Edwardian periods. Rape, however, could not be so simply paraphrased. Instead, during this period it is most likely to be presented as a vague crime 'against the laws of the Round Table'.[7] Chivalry, however anachronistically, is invoked not just to obscure gender-based violence, but also, I would argue, to provide a sense of safety in the form of 'the medieval' itself. It's no coincidence that the Wife of Bath's Tale is the only Arthurian tale, and adapters jumped at the chance to entice child readers with stories of the 'Blameless King', 'the soul of chivalry and honour'.[8]

In this vein, the inclusion of the Wife of Bath's Tale, however surprising given its violent content, aligns with the pervasive ethos of Victorian and Edwardian children's Chaucer: elevating Chaucer not in spite of, but *because* of his perceived status as a medieval root for contemporary Anglophone Christian ethno-nationalism. Victorian children's adapters, often devoutly Protestant women, tout Chaucer's religious credentials: more than being a 'thoroughly religious poet', he is presented with 'true Protestant feeling', which adapters frequently stretch to imply that Chaucer actively supported of John Wycliffe, the English reformer.[9] Adapters deploy the same alleged Christian moralism to excuse the violence of the Prioress's Tale, now recognised as a potently antisemitic version of the 'blood libel' story, in which a young Christian boy is murdered by Jews but which was nonetheless adapted eight times during this period. In two cases, the tale is accompanied by a disclaimer: 'The Jews', writes F.J. Harvey Darton in 1904, 'were greatly hated by the Christians in Europe…People were ready to believe almost anything evil of them'.[10] Neither adapter minces words, however, when it comes to the tale's violence: the murderer 'held [the boy] fast; then he cut his throat, and cast the dead body into a pit', and the guilty Jews are later 'tortured' and 'drawn by wild horses, and then hanged'.[11] Note, however, how Darton's disclaimer locates the problem not in the tale, but in the medieval mind: the brutal tale 'was neither strange nor painful to the pilgrims' because of their backwards views—views, it is implied, that Chaucer himself does not necessarily share.[12]

Perhaps even more than bloodless paraphrase or gendered omission, it is this elevated portrait of Chaucer that adapters deploy to render

Chaucer's violence 'safe'. Chaucer is pictured both a wise father and as a relatable, sunny child himself—'the sweetest and most childlike spirit in English song'.[13] The impression of Chaucer as a child is, on the one hand, patronising, as when Mary Haweis compares Middle English to toddlers' 'crude language'.[14] Yet it is also calculatedly unthreatening. As one children's biography puts it, 'Most of the other pages thought only of fighting, but Geoffrey often stole away to a quiet corner with a book'.[15] Children's Chaucer is a spirit both of his time and ahead of it—one whose approach to violence, readers glean, will be poetic, carefully measured, and morally upright: even 'those [stories] which are too coarse for modern taste are rather *naïve* than injurious'.[16] Chaucer's childlike persona, together with his paternal reputation as the 'Father of English Poetry', conjure a figure who is kindly and familiar. We are led to believe that any violence in his work must be justified—either by righteous morality or his own poetic obligation to capture his 'rough, unrefined times…so that he might hold it up to the world's repugnance'.[17] And while this may translate on the page to bloodless conflict or opacity, the very fact that these stories are adapted at all owes much to the idea of Chaucer's own imagined benevolence—however much that impression may be at odds with his text. As Mary Haweis put it, with pointed emphasis, in 1876: 'There is no clearer or *safer* exponent of the life of the 14th century, as far as he describes it, than Geoffrey Chaucer.'[18]

———————————————

Notes

[1] Charles Cowden Clarke, *Tales from Chaucer, in Prose. Designed Chiefly for the Use of Young Persons* (London, 1833), pp. iii–iv.

[2] Mary Eliza Haweis, *Chaucer for Children: A Golden Key* (1876; repr., London, 1877), p. ix.

[3] Line numbers are from *The Canterbury Tales* as printed in Geoffrey Chaucer, *The Riverside Chaucer*, ed. Larry D. Benson, Third Edition (Oxford, 2008).

[4] *Tales from Chaucer*, Gowans's Copyright Series 1 (London and Glasgow, 1909), p. 17.

[5] David Murray Smith, *Tales of Chivalry and Romance* (London, 1869), p. 15.

[6] Mary Seymour, *Chaucer's Stories Simply Told, With Illustrations* (London, 1884), p. 28.

[7] Clara L. Thomson, *Tales from Chaucer* (London, 1903), p. 192.

[8] William Calder, *Chaucer's Canterbury Pilgrimage*, First Edition (Edinburgh and London, 1892), p. 152; W.T. Stead, *Stories from Chaucer, Being the Canterbury Tales in Simple Language for Children*, Books for the Bairns 83 (London, 1903), p. 17.

[9] Haweis, *Chaucer for Children*, p. x; cf. F.J. Furnivall, "Introduction," in *Tales of the Canterbury Pilgrims: Retold from Chaucer & Others*, by F.J. Harvey Darton, Second Edition (1904; repr., London, 1904), p. iv.

[10] F.J. Harvey Darton, *Tales of the Canterbury Pilgrims: Retold from Chaucer & Others* (London, 1904), p. 98; cf. John Alexander Hammerton, "The Story of Famous Books: Chaucer's *Canterbury Tales*," in *The Children's Encyclopædia*, ed. Arthur Mee (London, 1908), p. 214.

[11] Darton, *Canterbury Pilgrims*, pp. 101–2.

[12] Darton, *Canterbury Pilgrims*, p. 98.

[13] Katharine Lee Bates, *The Story of Chaucer's Canterbury Pilgrims Retold for Children*, Canterbury Classics (New York; Chicago; London, 1909), p. 10.

[14] *Chaucer for Children*, p. ix.

[15] *Highroads of Literature*, The Royal School Series, III. The Morning Star (1919; repr., London, Edinburgh, and New York, 1921), p. 23.

[16] Haweis, *Chaucer for Children*, p. x.

[17] Seymour, *Chaucer*, p. xii.

[18] *Chaucer for Children*, p. x.

Books Displayed
Mary Boyle

1843   Gustav Pfizer, *Der Nibelungen Noth*, Stuttgart.
        The Bodleian Libraries, University of Oxford: 38.M.13

This verse translation of the *Nibelungenlied* into modern German had an enduring legacy because of its visual layout. It includes a large number of woodcuts produced by the Xylographische Anstalt von Kaspar Braun & [Georg] von Dessauer, based on illustrations by Julius Schnorr von Carolsfeld and Eugen Neureuther. Beginning in the 1820s, Schnorr created a series of frescoes to decorate the walls and ceilings of a series of rooms in the royal palace of King Ludwig I in Munich, and these had a second life as woodcuts. The woodcuts, as included by Pfizer, along with the related page design, found their way directly into a number of other *Nibelungenlied* translations, and were enormously influential for further *Nibelungenlied* translators and adapters.

Available online:
http://dbooks.bodleian.ox.ac.uk/books/PDFs/N10974752.pdf

★★

1848   Anonymous, *The Heroic Life and Exploits of Siegfried the Dragon Slayer: An Old German Story*, illustrated by Wilhelm Kaulbach, London.

The Bodleian Libraries, University of Oxford: FIEDLER.G.550 (Taylorian exhibition) | Johnson d. 4468 (online exhibition)

This is a remarkably early example of an English-language publication aimed at children—most post-date the English premiere of Wagner's *Ring des Nibelungen*. It is based on a prior German publication, and primarily adapts the legends of Siegfried which do not appear in the *Nibelungenlied*, though it alludes to the events of that text, including—briefly—Kriemhild's revenge at the end. Editions were printed both with the plates in black and white and in colour.

Available online:

http://dbooks.bodleian.ox.ac.uk/books/PDFs/N10974976.pdf

**

1880   Lydia Hands, *Golden Threads from an Ancient Loom. Das Nibelunglied, adapted to the use of young readers*, with fourteen wood engravings by Julius Schnorr, of Carolsfeld, London.

Private loan | Printed reproduction in Taylorian exhibition from The Bodleian Libraries, University of Oxford: (OC) 250 d.150

Golden Threads is the first of the flood of children's adaptations of *Nibelungen*-related material in the later nineteenth and early twentieth centuries. It is unusually complete amongst works aimed at children in adapting the full narrative, albeit with some obfuscation. The narrative was augmented with additional legends of Siegfried, all found in Thomas Carlyle's essay, and Carlyle was the dedicatee. The woodcuts and the corresponding layout are a selection from those which originally appeared in Pfizer's *Der Nibelungen Noth* (1843), though Hands discovered them in a translation by Karl Simrock, published in 1873. She casts Kriemhild as driven to violence by madness—an excuse for violent women also used in legal contexts.

Available online:

http://dbooks.bodleian.ox.ac.uk/books/PDFs/600055796.pdf

**

1883   James Baldwin, illustrated by Howard Pyle, *The Story of Siegfried*, London.

The Bodleian Libraries, University of Oxford: 930 d.268 (Taylorian exhibition) | The Bodleian Libraries, University of Oxford: (OC) 251 k.796 (online exhibition)

The Story of Siegfried was also intended for a young audience; in fact, Baldwin dedicated it to his three children. His intention was only to retell legends of Siegfried himself, and he drew on the *Nibelungenlied*, the *Völsunga Saga*, the *Eddas*, and 'some of the minor legends', of which he probably learned from Carlyle. He also admits to having employed his own imagination. He ends his retelling with the theft of the treasure, but alludes in his afterword to Kriemhild's revenge. The images appear to be original to Baldwin's publication, and continued to appear in numerous reprints.

Note: The copy displayed in the Taylorian exhibition is the 1931 reprint.

Available online:

http://dbooks.bodleian.ox.ac.uk/books/PDFs/600073169.pdf

**

1883   *Epics and Romances of the Middle Ages*, adapted from the work of Dr W. Wägner by M.W. MacDowall, and edited by W.S.W. Anson, London.

The Bodleian Libraries, University of Oxford: 930 e.13

This is essentially a translation of Wilhelm Wägner's *Deutsche Heldensagen* (Leipzig and Berlin, 1881), and the introduction appeals to 'our common ancestry' as German and English. It includes an array of mostly heroic literature, including adaptations of both the *Nibelungen* material and *Beowulf*. The images are reproductions of those in Wägner's publication, where they are listed as based on illustrations by Hermann Vogel.

Note: The copy displayed is the second edition, printed in 1884.

Available online:

http://dbooks.bodleian.ox.ac.uk/books/PDFs/600064973.pdf

**

1897   Margaret Armour, *The Fall of the Nibelungs*, illustrated and decorated by W.B. MacDougall, London.

The Bodleian Libraries, University of Oxford: FIEDLER.G.600 (Taylorian exhibition) | The Bodleian Libraries, University of Oxford: 28849 e.60 (Taylorian and online exhibitions)

Armour's *Fall of the Nibelungs* is relatively unusual amongst complete translations of the *Nibelungenlied* into English in being illustrated— and her illustrator was her husband. It was more common for illustrations to appear in adaptations. Translators were often overtly concerned to present their work as scholarly, and this was often taken to preclude images. Armour intended her translation to be a close rendering of the medieval text in modern English prose, and it was well received as such. Like most nineteenth-century anglophone translators, however, she also made use of a modern German translation, in this case a parallel text edition by Karl Simrock, which offered access to the Middle High German alongside a modern German text.

Available online:

https://archive.org/details/cu31924026159990

**

1898   Zénaïde Alexeïevna Ragozin, *Siegfried, the Hero of the North, and Beowulf, the Hero of the Anglo-Saxons,* illustrated by George T. Tobin, New York.

The Bodleian Libraries, University of Oxford: 3967 e.54

Ragozin, a Russian expatriate in the United States, produced volumes for children to represent the 'national epics' of various regions. For the 'North', her publications included this volume, in which she paired *Beowulf* and the *Nibelungenlied*. She regarded the latter as 'the masterpiece of a race'. Ragozin's objective was to entertain and to instruct, and she adapted the full narrative, though she made an effort to reduce Kriemhild's culpability for much of the violence. The book contains eight black and white plates by George T. Tobin (1864–1956).

Note: This publication is not included in the online exhibition for copyright reasons.

Available online:

https://babel.hathitrust.org/cgi/pt?id=coo1.ark:/13960/t14m9rf6r&view=1up&seq=13

**

1907   Anonymous, *The Linden Leaf; or, The Story of Siegfried. Retold from the Nibelungen Lied*, London.

The Bodleian Libraries, University of Oxford: 28849 f.4

This is another publication aimed at a young audience and it includes eight brightly coloured illustrations, which seem to be signed 'Waugh'. It adapts the first half of the *Nibelungenlied*, also making brief reference to some other legends of Siegfried's youth. It ends after Siegfried's murder and, although it alludes to Kriemhild's desire to 'punish his murderer', there is no more explicit reference to her vengeance, and readers are assured that Hagen ultimately meets a hero's death, having 'fully atoned for his sins'.

Note: This publication is not included in the online exhibition for copyright reasons.

**

1907   Tho[ma]s Cartwright, *Sigurd the Dragon-Slayer, A Twice-Told Tale*, London.

The Bodleian Libraries, University of Oxford: 930 f.107

Cartwright offers a retelling for children, first of the Norse material 'as fashioned ... for the delight of our sea-roving Viking forefathers', and then of the *Nibelungenlied*, 'for which we are indebted to our cousins, the Germans'. The text of the latter section is taken entirely from Thomas Carlyle. In addition to eight colour plates, there are numerous black and white engravings. No details are given for the illustrator(s), but some of the black and white images are accompanied by the monogram 'I.B.'. It does not appear that on this occasion Cartwright worked with Patten Wilson, who illustrated his

Brave Beowulf in the same series.

Note: This publication is not included in the online exhibition for copyright reasons.

Available online:
https://babel.hathitrust.org/cgi/pt?id=uva.x001862935&view=1up&seq=12

**

1908   Mary MacGregor, *Stories of Siegfried, told to the children*, with pictures by Granville Fell, London.
Private loan.

Unusually, this children's adaptation does not appeal to a shared Germanic heritage, but draws a distinction between 'the German hero', Siegfried, and 'your French and English heroes'. MacGregor draws on Norse material to an extent, but her primary source is the first half of the *Nibelungenlied*. She deals with the second half of the narrative in the final page, noting that Siegfried's death was eventually 'avenged by Queen Kriemhild', but implies that the violence was carried out only by men, and omits Kriemhild's own fate. There are eight colour plates by Granville Fell. The publication is undated, but 1908 is the usual date given.

**

1910   Dora Ford Madeley, *The Heroic Life and Exploits of Siegfried the Dragon-Slayer. An Old Story of the North*, illustrated by Stephen Reid, London.

The Bodleian Libraries, University of Oxford: 930 e.414

As the title suggests, this publication was based closely on the anonymous 1848 publication illustrated by Kaulbach. The text was revised, and a whole new series of colour illustrations by Stephen Reid (1873–1948) was substituted. One of Ford Madeley's changes was to remove the already brief allusion to Kriemhild's revenge for Siegfried's death at the end of the work.

**

1911   Anonymous, *Siegfried and Kriemhild. A Story of Passion and Revenge*, illustrated by Frank C. Papé, London.

The Bodleian Libraries, University of Oxford: 28849 d.25

This is a relatively thorough retelling of the *Nibelungenlied* for children, with the framing device that it is told in a tavern in Worms in 1460. The Kriemhild of this adaptation is ultimately even more violent than the medieval Kriemhild, killing her brother, as well as Hagen, herself, but the author follows Lydia Hands in implying that her actions are the result of madness. The text is accompanied by eight colour plates by Frank Cheyne Papé (1878-1972).

Note: This publication is not included in the online exhibition for copyright reasons.

**

1912   Donald Mackenzie, *Teutonic Myths and Legends*, London.

The Bodleian Libraries, University of Oxford: 930 e.541

Mackenzie's collection of shortened retellings described itself as 'an introduction to the *Eddas* and Sagas, *Beowulf*, *The Nibelungenlied*. etc'. It was aimed at adults and, like other similar publications, included a number of images previously published elsewhere. The image displayed is based on one of Julius Schnorr von Carolsfeld's frescoes—and notably not a woodcut version. The publication is undated, but 1912 is the usual date given.

**

1913   G. Hugelshofer and A.F.C Vilmar, *Analysis of the Nibelungenlied as contained in the Geschichte der Deutschen [sic] National-Litteratur*, London.

The Bodleian Libraries, University of Oxford: 28849 f.6

G.E. Hugelshofer was a Modern Languages teacher in Dumfries, who adapted A.F.C. Vilmar's summary of the *Nibelungenlied* (originally published in 1846) to create an aid to language teaching. He added vocabulary exercises, passages for translation, and notes, as well as modernising the spelling. Hugelshofer also included various images which had previously been published elsewhere. The image displayed in the exhibition is a woodcut produced by the

Xylographische Anstalt von Kaspar Braun & [Georg] von Dessauer, and based on an illustration by Alfred Rethel.

'Death of Siegfried' (detail)
Lydia Hands, *Golden Threads from an Ancient Loom. Das Nibelunglied, adapted to the use of young readers*, with fourteen wood engravings by Julius Schnorr, of Carolsfeld, London, 1880, frontispiece.
Private loan.

Panels
Mary Boyle

Panel 1: Doomed Heroes

Here we see heroes who will not go on to triumph, whether they are to meet their deaths in a blaze of glory, or as a result of betrayal. Two images show Hagen's cowardly murder of the great hero, Siegfried, whose strength and invulnerability mean that he can only be destroyed through deception. One image shows Hagen's desperate and violent attempt to disprove a dreadful prophecy that all but one of the Burgundians are doomed, should they continue with their journey. The other images depict the Burgundian warriors, fighting unrelentingly in the face of certain death. This panel shows courage and pathos, bravery and treachery, and it tells a complex tale: Hagen is the aggressor in several of the images, yet one of the valiant warriors fighting against the odds in the others.

The *Nibelungenlied* was viewed as the German national epic, but anglophone writers often also staked their own claims to it. The underdog's struggle against immeasurable odds is a frequent feature of national narratives, including in this country, and we see here warriors depicted at their defining moment, characterised not necessarily by their virtues or achievements, but by their most desperate experiences.

Panel 2: Women and Violence

The chief architect of much of the violence in the *Nibelungenlied* is the beautiful Queen Kriemhild, seeking revenge for Siegfried's death. This was a source of difficulty for many nineteenth-century adapters, who sought variously to make an example of her, to make excuses for her, or to rehabilitate her entirely. But even where there was an attempt to explain her actions, the temptation to depict her at her most transgressive—brandishing the decapitated head of her brother—was almost irresistible. And the scale of that transgression also gave illustrators licence to depict Kriemhild's own violent death, with her final victim, Hagen, lying at her feet.

Kriemhild is not the only violent woman in the *Nibelungen* material. Her sister-in-law, Brünhild, who is a valkyrie in both Norse legend and Wagner's *Ring*, was possessed of immense physical strength before her marriage, and children's books in particular often include images of her with her spear. In contrast to Kriemhild, there is ultimately no direct victim of Brünhild's violence, but the illustrators commonly show the fear of the male heroes, as they cower behind a shield, emphasising the threat offered by a physically strong woman.

Panel 3: Fantasy Violence

In this panel, we see the continuities between nineteenth-century medievalism and more recent medievalist fantasy material, particularly onscreen (e.g. *Game of Thrones*, *The Hobbit*, *Merlin*, *Harry Potter*). Siegfried's fight with the dragon takes place entirely off-stage in the *Nibelungenlied*, and it is only mentioned once or twice in passing. It is, though, far more prominent in other traditions, and its appeal to illustrators, especially of children's adaptations, needs no explanation.

These versions for younger readers frequently avoid adapting, or fully adapting, the second half of the narrative, with its focus on brutal vengeance. This has the effect of rebalancing the story into one focused entirely on Siegfried's heroics, with Kriemhild simply functioning as a mild and beautiful love interest. Such adaptations also tend to bring in material which is omitted from, or played down in, the *Nibelungenlied* itself. While Siegfried's violent death prevents such adaptations from culminating in a traditionally child-friendly happy ending, their emphasis on fantasy elements like the dragon gives them a fairy-tale quality which we recognise today.

Exhibits
Mary Boyle

Panel 1: Doomed Heroes
Siegfried's Murder

> 'As Lord Siegfried bent to drink from the fountain, Hagen shot him through the cross on his back, so that his heart's blood sprang from the wound on to Hagen's clothes. A hero never did a worse deed.'
>
> *The Nibelungenlied*, stanza 981

Neither the medieval author nor the later adapters and illustrators hid their feelings: the treacherous stabbing in the back of an unarmed hero was a uniquely infamous and shameful action.

Displayed in the Taylorian exhibition, but not in the online exhibition or catalogue for copyright reasons:

'Death of Siegfried'
Zénaïde Alexeïevna Ragozin, *Siegfried, the Hero of the North, and Beowulf, the Hero of the Anglo-Saxons*, illustrated by George T. Tobin, New York, 1908, facing p. 102.
The Bodleian Libraries, University of Oxford: 3967 e.54

'Hagen kills Siegfried'
Thomas Cartwright, *Sigurd the Dragon-Slayer, A Twice-Told Tale* (London, 1907), p. 82.
The Bodleian Libraries, University of Oxford: 930 f.107

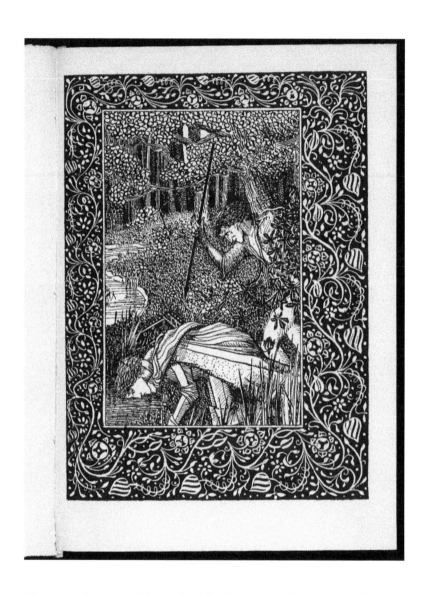

Margaret Armour, *The Fall of the Nibelungs*, illustrated and decorated by W.B. MacDougall, London, 1897.
The Bodleian Libraries, University of Oxford: 28849 e.60. Online exhibition only.

'While Siegfried drank the cool, clear water, Hagen stabbed him'
Mary MacGregor, *Stories of Siegfried, told to the children*, with pictures
by Granville Fell, London, c. 1908, facing p. 114.
Private loan. Online exhibition only.

Hagen attempts to drown the chaplain

'I wanted to prove the wild water women lied when they said none of us but the chaplain would return home, so I tried to drown him'

The Nibelungenlied, stanza 1589

Hagen, Siegfried's killer, attempts to disprove a prophecy that only the chaplain will return home alive by ensuring he doesn't. The priest survives, and Hagen and his comrades press on, knowing their fate. The image captures both aggressor's and victim's despair.

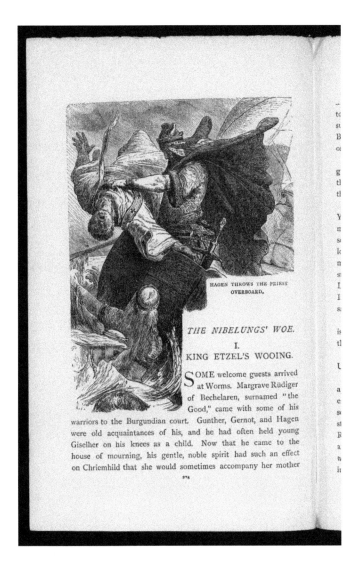

HAGEN THROWS THE PRIEST
OVERBOARD.

THE NIBELUNGS' WOE.

I.

KING ETZEL'S WOOING.

SOME welcome guests arrived at Worms. Margrave Rüdiger of Bechelaren, surnamed "the Good," came with some of his warriors to the Burgundian court. Gunther, Gernot, and Hagen were old acquaintances of his, and he had often held young Giselher on his knees as a child. Now that he came to the house of mourning, his gentle, noble spirit had such an effect on Chriemhild that she would sometimes accompany her mother

274

Epics and Romances of the Middle Ages, adapted from the work of Dr W. Wägner by M.W. MacDowall, and edited by W.S.W. Anson, London, 1884, 2nd edn. Images based on illustrations by Hermann Vogel and reproduced from Wilhelm Wägner, *Deutscher Heldensagen*, Leipzig and Berlin, 1881, p. 274.
The Bodleian Libraries, University of Oxford: 930 e.13

Battle at the Huns' Court

'Then they took 7000 corpses to the door, and threw them outside, where they fell down the stairs'

The Nibelungenlied, stanza 2013

The frantic battle at the Huns' court showcases the complexity of the *Nibelungenlied*. Characters like Hagen, who have behaved shamefully, now fight with honour against horrific odds. The death toll is such that even the most graphic of these images falls short of its scale.

'The fight on the stairs of Etzel's palace'
Donald Mackenzie, *Teutonic Myths and Legends*, London, c. 1912,
between pp. 400–401.
The Bodleian Libraries, University of Oxford: 930 e.541

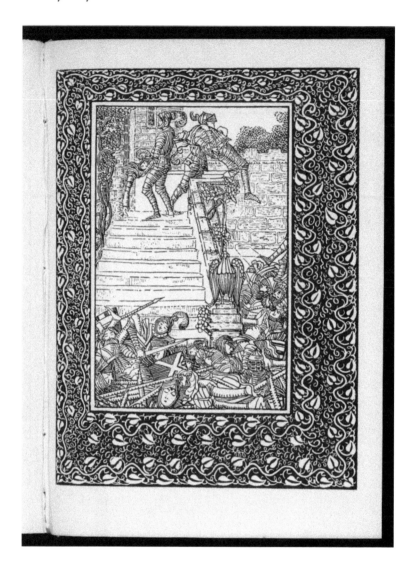

Margaret Armour, *The Fall of the Nibelungs*, illustrated and decorated by W.B. MacDougall, London, 1897, facing p. 222.
The Bodleian Libraries, University of Oxford: FIEDLER.G.600 (Taylorian exhibition) | The Bodleian Libraries, University of Oxford: 28849 e.60 (reproduction)

THE SLAUGHTER IN THE BANQUET HALL.

'The slaughter in the banquet hall'
Lydia Hands, *Golden Threads from an Ancient Loom. Das Nibelunglied, adapted to the use of young readers* with fourteen wood engravings by Julius Schnorr, of Carolsfeld, London, 1880, p. 61.
Private loan. Online exhibition only.

Panel 2: Women and Violence

Kriemhild holding Gunther's severed head

'Then she commanded her brother's life to be taken. His head was cut off, and she carried it by its hair before the hero of Tronje'

The Nibelungenlied, stanza 2369

Many adapters were struck by this moment, and chose to depict it, or reprint famous depictions, to demonstrate how outrageous Kriemhild's behaviour was. The event was often placed in a prominent position, at the start of a section, or as a frontispiece.

Displayed in the Taylorian exhibition, but not in the online exhibition or catalogue for copyright reasons:

'Kriemhild outfaces Hagen'
Anonymous, *Siegfried and Kriemhild. A Story of Passion and Revenge*, illustrated by Frank C. Papé, London, 1911, frontispiece.
The Bodleian Libraries, University of Oxford: 28849 d.25.

Gustav Pfizer, *Der Nibelungen Noth*, with woodcuts by the
Xylographische Anstalt von Kaspar Braun & [Georg] von Dessauer,
based on illustrations by Julius Schnorr von Carolsfeld and Eugen
Neureuther, Stuttgart, 1843, p. 427.
The Bodleian Libraries, University of Oxford: 38.M.13

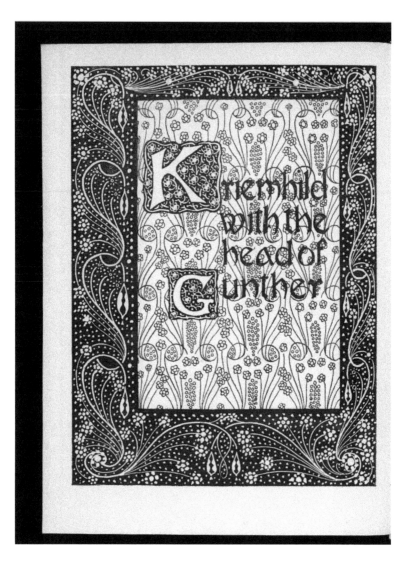

'Kriemhild with the head of Gunther'
Margaret Armour, *The Fall of the Nibelungs*, illustrated and decorated by W.B. MacDougall, London, 1897, between pp. 126-127. The Bodleian Libraries, University of Oxford: 28849 e.60

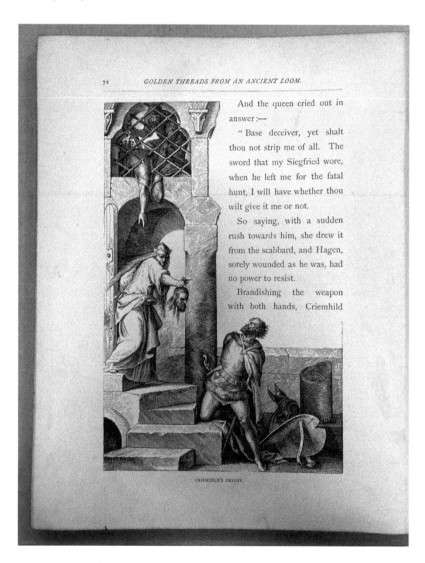

'Criemhild's frenzy'

Lydia Hands, *Golden Threads from an Ancient Loom. Das Nibe-lunglied, adapted to the use of young readers*, with fourteen wood en-gravings by Julius Schnorr, of Carolsfeld, London, 1880, p. 72. Private loan.

Kriemhild's death

'How can the greatest knight be lying dead at a woman's hands? ... She shall not benefit from daring to slay him.'
The Nibelungenlied, stanzas 2374-75

This depiction of active violence against a woman is deliberately shocking: Kriemhild's wickedness, evidenced by the body of her final victim at her feet, allows her brutal death to be illustrated. Both these books, for younger audiences, incorporate reproductions of older images, originally directed at adults.

'Wie Hagen und Kriemhild erschlagen wurden'
G. Hugelshofer and A.F.C Vilmar, *Analysis of the Nibelungenlied as
contained in the Geschichte der Deutschen [sic] National-Litteratur*,
London, 1913, facing p. 72. Woodcut based on an illustration by
Alfred Rethel.
The Bodleian Libraries, University of Oxford: 28849 f.6

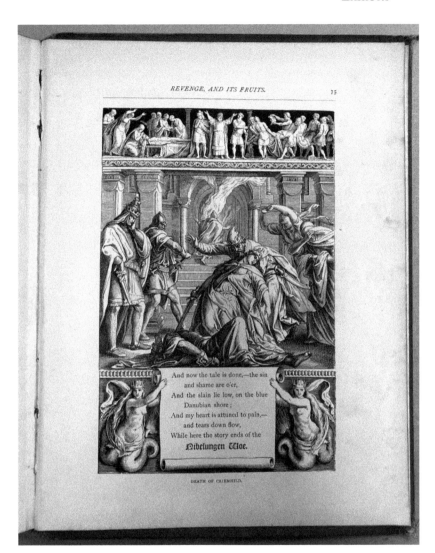

'Death of Criemhild'
Lydia Hands, *Golden Threads from an Ancient Loom. Das Nibelunglied, adapted to the use of young readers*, with fourteen wood engravings by Julius Schnorr, of Carolsfeld, London, 1880. The woodcuts are a selection from Pfizer (1843), p. 75.
Private loan. Online exhibition only.

Brünhild hurls her spear

'The remarkable maiden threw the spear with great force'

The Nibelungenlied, stanza 456

Children's adaptations often include images of the supernaturally strong warrior queen, Brünhild. Here, in a trial of strength for her hand in marriage, she prepares to hurl a spear at a shield, behind which are sheltering Gunther and—unbeknownst to Brünhild—an invisible Siegfried, who will win the trial on Gunther's behalf.

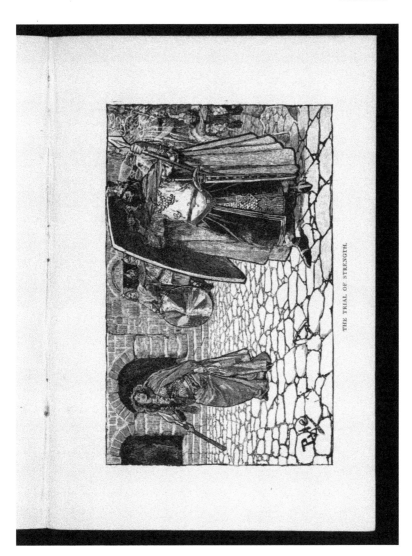

'The Trial of Strength'
James Baldwin, illustrated by Howard Pyle, *The Story of Siegfried*,
London, 1883, repr. 1931), p. 180.
The Bodleian Libraries, University of Oxford: 930 d.268 | The
Bodleian Libraries, University of Oxford: (OC) 251 k.796) (reproduction)

The maiden hurled her spear (page 76)

'The maiden hurled her spear'
Mary MacGregor, *Stories of Siegfried, told to the children*, with pictures by Granville Fell, London, c. 1908, facing p. 76.
Private loan. Online exhibition only.

Fantasy Violence

Siegfried fights the dragon

> 'The hero slew a dragon. He bathed in its blood: his skin
> grew horn-hard, so no weapon can cut him'
>
> *The Nibelungenlied*, stanza 100

Here we see five eye-catching depictions of Siegfried's combat with the dragon, which is mentioned only in passing in the *Nibelungenlied*. All five are aimed at children, and in two, Siegfried appears close to the audience's age—much like the heroes of many modern Young Adult fantasy books.

Displayed in the Taylorian exhibition, but not in the online exhibition or catalogue for copyright reasons:

'The boy Siegfried kills the dragon'
Anonymous, *The Linden Leaf; or, The Story of Siegfried. Retold from the Nibelungen Lied*, London, 1907.
The Bodleian Libraries, University of Oxford: 28849 f.4

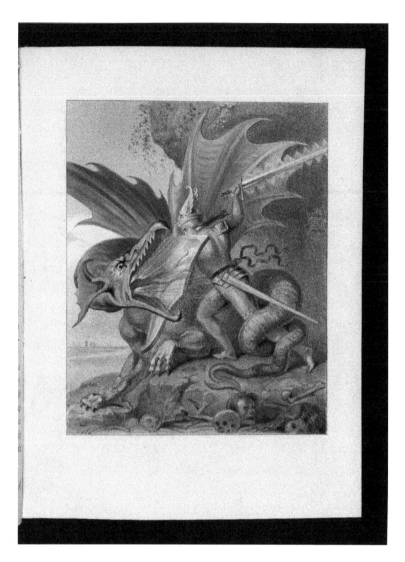

Anonymous, *The Heroic Life and Exploits of Siegfried the Dragon Slayer: An Old German Story*, illustrated by Wilhelm Kaulbach, London, 1848, facing p. 108.
The Bodleian Libraries, University of Oxford: FIEDLER.G.550 l
The Bodleian Libraries, University of Oxford: Johnson d. 4468 (reproduction)

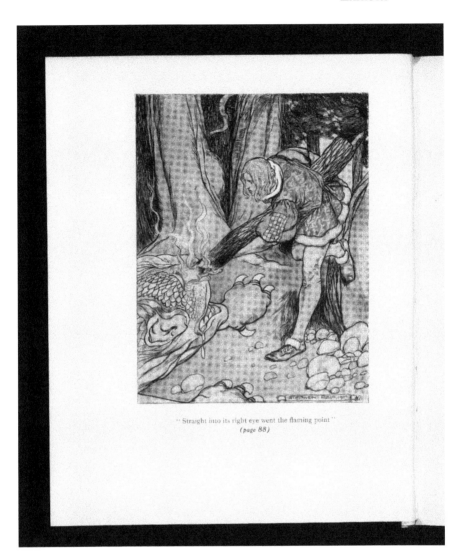

" Straight into its right eye went the flaming point "
(page 88)

'Straight into its right eye went the flaming point'
Dora Ford Madeley, *The Heroic Life and Exploits of Siegfried the Dragon-Slayer. An Old Story of the North*, illustrated by Stephen Reid, London, 1910, frontispiece.
The Bodleian Libraries, University of Oxford: 930 e.414.

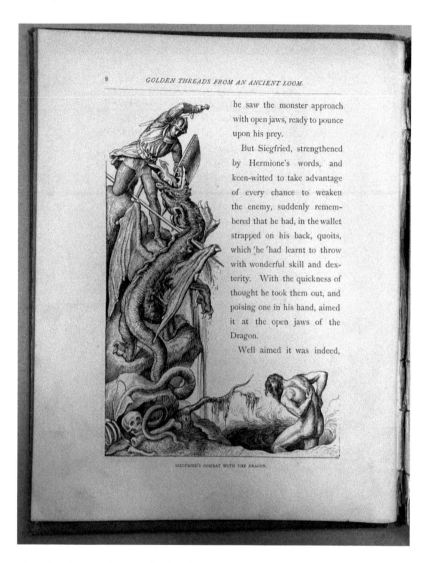

he saw the monster approach with open jaws, ready to pounce upon his prey.

But Siegfried, strengthened by Hermione's words, and keen-witted to take advantage of every chance to weaken the enemy, suddenly remembered that he had, in the wallet strapped on his back, quoits, which 'he 'had learnt to throw with wonderful skill and dexterity. With the quickness of thought he took them out, and poising one in his hand, aimed it at the open jaws of the Dragon.

Well aimed it was indeed,

SIEGFRIED'S COMBAT WITH THE DRAGON.

'Siegfried's combat with the dragon'
Lydia Hands, *Golden Threads from an Ancient Loom. Das Nibelunglied, adapted to the use of young readers* with fourteen wood engravings by Julius Schnorr, of Carolsfeld, London, 1880, p. 8.
Private loan | The Bodleian Libraries, University of Oxford: (OC) 250 d.150 (Taylorian exhibition printed reproduction)

'I will kill thee, for in truth thou art an ugly monster'
Mary MacGregor, *Stories of Siegfried, told to the children*, with pictures by Granville Fell, London, c. 1908, facing p. 8.
Private loan.

CPSIA information can be obtained
at www.ICGtesting.com
Printed in the USA
BVHW020722191122
652269BV00021B/667

9 781838 464103